greek

all your favourite greek recipes

THE AUSTRALIAN Women's Weekly

CONTENTS

greek essentials	4
mezze	6
soups & salads	18
seafood	26
chicken & rabbit	34
lamb & goat	40
vegetable dishes	54
sweets	60
glossary	74
conversion chart	77
index	78

AUSTRALIAN CUP AND
SPOON MEASUREMENTS
ARE METRIC.
A CONVERSION CHART
APPEARS ON PAGE 77.

From mountainous terrain to seaside villages, the topography of Greece has had a great influence on its food – salads, lamb, goat, cheese, mezze plates and seafood. Greek food encourages entertaining and celebration, and this book is full of all the favourites.

Pamela Clark

Food Director

FETTA CHEESE

Traditionally made with sheep's milk, now most often cow's milk. It is shaped into large blocks which are salted, sliced and salted again, then packed in whey for a month or so. It ends up firm, sharp-flavoured and salty. Packed in brine, it should be eaten within a day or two of purchase.

HALOUMI CHEESE

This Cypriot cheese is often used in Greek cooking. It's a firm, traditionally sheep's-milk cheese (goat's or cow's-milk varieties also available) with a minty, salty flavour; it does not break down when cooked, however it should be eaten while still warm as it becomes tough and rubbery on cooling.

KALAMATA OLIVES

Large black olives with a firm flesh and meaty flavour; named after the city of Kalamata in Greece. They are available preserved in vinegar or olive oil, and whole or pitted.

RIGANI

Dried Greek oregano, often sold in bunches. Store dried herbs away from heat or light in airtight packets or containers; do not store in the fridge as transferring between a cold fridge and warm kitchen can cause condensation inside the packet and spoil its contents.

GREEK ESSENTIALS

VINE LEAVES

Fresh or preserved grapevine leaves, used for wrapping fillings (dolmades) or as lining for dishes with savoury mixtures. Preserved leaves are packed in brine so should be rinsed and dried before use. Fresh leaves should be softened in boiling water for a minute until pliable, then dried.

TAHINI

A sesame seed paste; used in dips such as baba ghanoush (eggplant dip) and hummus (chickpea dip). It is available from health food stores, the health food section in most supermarkets and Middle Eastern food stores.

GREEK-STYLE YOGURT

This yogurt has been strained in a cloth (traditionally muslin), to remove the whey and to give it a creamy consistency. It's ideal for use in dips and dressings.

FILLO PASTRY

Paper-thin sheets of raw pastry; are used by brushing with oil or melted butter and stacking one on another, then cutting and folding as the recipe directs. This creates a layered, crackling-crisp, airy crust or wrapping for small pastries such as spanakopita.

DOLMADES

prep + cook time 3 hours (+ standing) **serves** 10
nutritional count per serving 7.6g total fat
(1.6g saturated fat); 690kJ (165 cal);
14.9g carbohydrate; 7.7g protein; 3.2g fibre

2 tablespoons olive oil
2 medium brown onions (300g),
   chopped finely
155g (5 ounces) lean minced (ground) lamb
¾ cup (150g) white long-grain rice
2 tablespoons pine nuts
½ cup finely chopped fresh flat-leaf parsley
2 tablespoons each finely chopped
   fresh dill and mint
¼ cup (60ml) lemon juice
2 cups (500ml) water
500g (1 pound) preserved vine leaves
¾ cup (200g) yogurt

1 Heat oil in large saucepan; cook onion,
stirring, until softened. Add lamb; cook, stirring,
until browned. Stir in rice and nuts. Add herbs,
2 tablespoons of the juice and half the water;
bring to the boil. Reduce heat; simmer, covered,
10 minutes or until water is absorbed and rice
is partially cooked. Season. Cool.
2 Rinse vine leaves under cold water; drain well.
3 Place a vine leaf, smooth-side down on
bench, trim large stem. Place a heaped
teaspoon of rice mixture in centre. Fold stem
end and sides over filling; roll up firmly.
4 Line medium heavy-based saucepan with a
few vine leaves; place rolls, close together,
seam-side down, on leaves.
5 Pour over the remaining water; cover rolls
with any remaining leaves. Place a plate on top
of leaves to weigh down rolls. Cover pan tightly,
bring to the boil. Reduce heat; simmer, over
very low heat, 1½ hours. Remove from heat;
stand, covered, about 2 hours or until liquid
has been absorbed.
6 Serve dolmades with combined yogurt and
remaining juice.

tip Preserved vine leaves are packed in brine so
should be rinsed and dried before use. Fresh leaves
should be softened in boiling water for a minute until
pliable, then dried.

MEZZE

FRIED CHILLI PRAWNS WITH GARLIC AND LEMON YOGURT

prep + cook time **20 minutes** serves **6**
nutritional count per serving **8.2g total fat**
(2.7g saturated fat); 866kJ (207 cal);
12.9g carbohydrate; 20g protein; 0.7g fibre

vegetable oil, for deep-frying
500g (1 pound) uncooked small
  prawns (shrimp)
1 cup (150g) plain (all-purpose) flour
1 teaspoon ground chilli
garlic and lemon yogurt
¾ cup (210g) greek-style yogurt
1 clove garlic, crushed
1 teaspoon finely grated lemon rind
1 tablespoon lemon juice

1 Make garlic and lemon yogurt.
2 Heat vegetable oil in medium saucepan
or wok. Toss unshelled prawns in combined
flour and chilli; shake away excess.
3 Deep-fry prawns, in batches, until browned
lightly. Drain on absorbent paper. Season with
salt and a little extra ground chilli to taste.
4 Serve prawns with yogurt and lemon wedges.
garlic and lemon yogurt Combine ingredients
in small bowl; season to taste.

BARBECUED
BABY OCTOPUS

prep + cook time **25 minutes** (+ refrigeration) serves **6**
nutritional count per serving **13.4g total fat**
(1.7g saturated fat); 982kJ (235 cal);
1g carbohydrate; 27.6g protein; 0.2g fibre

Clean 1kg (2 pounds) baby octopus; discard
eyes and beaks. Combine octopus with ⅓ cup
lemon juice, ⅓ cup olive oil, 2 crushed garlic
cloves and 2 teaspoons rigani in medium bowl.
Cover; refrigerate 3 hours or overnight. Drain
octopus; discard marinade. Cook octopus
on heated oiled grill plate (or grill or barbecue)
until tender.

tips Ask the fishmonger to clean the baby octopus for
you. Don't overcook baby octopus or it will be tough.
It's ready as soon as it changes colour.
serving suggestion Lemon wedges and tzatziki (page 17).

FRIED
LAMB MEATBALLS

prep + cook time **20 minutes** makes **24**
nutritional count per meatball **4g total fat**
(1.4g saturated fat); 225kJ (54 cal);
0.8g carbohydrate; 3.6g protein; 0.1g fibre

Combine 300g (10 ounces) minced (ground)
lamb with 1 finely chopped small brown onion,
60g (2 ounces) crumbled fetta cheese, ½ cup
stale breadcrumbs, 1 egg and 2 tablespoons
finely chopped fresh mint in medium bowl;
season. Roll level tablespoons of mixture into
balls. Heat 2 tablespoons olive oil in large frying
pan; cook balls, in batches, until browned and
cooked through. Drain on absorbent paper.

tips To shape the meatballs well, it's important to
chop the onion finely. The secret to round meatballs is
to make a circular movement with the pan to roll the
meatballs around while they cook.
serving suggestion Tzatziki (page 17).

DEEP-FRIED EGGPLANT
WITH HERB SAUCE

prep + cook time **20 minutes** makes **20 slices**
nutritional count per slice **5.3g total fat**
(0.8g saturated fat); 230kJ (55 cal);
1.6g carbohydrate; 0.5g protein; 1g fibre

To make herb sauce, blend or process 1 cup
each loosely packed fresh oregano and flat-leaf
parsley leaves, ⅓ cup olive oil, 2 crushed cloves
garlic, 1 teaspoon finely grated lemon rind and
1 tablespoon lemon juice until smooth; season
to taste. Cut 2 medium eggplant into 10 slices
each. Season 2 tablespoons plain (all-purpose)
flour with salt and pepper. Toss eggplant in
flour, shake away excess. Heat vegetable oil in
medium saucepan or wok; deep-fry eggplant,
in batches, until browned and tender. Remove
from pan; drain on absorbent paper. Serve
eggplant drizzled with sauce.

tips Store sauce in airtight container in refrigerator.
This sauce also goes well with deep-fried zucchini
balls (page 15).

DEEP-FRIED
BABY CALAMARI

prep + cook time **15 minutes** serves **4**
nutritional count per serving **4g total fat**
(0.6g saturated fat); 425kJ (100 cal);
6.4g carbohydrate; 9.9g protein; 0.4g fibre

Slice 500g (1 pound) cleaned baby calamari
into thin rings. Season ⅓ cup plain (all-purpose)
flour with salt and pepper. Toss calamari in flour
mixture; shake away excess. Heat vegetable
oil in medium saucepan or wok; deep-fry
calamari, in batches, until browned lightly and
tender. Drain on absorbent paper. Sprinkle with
2 teaspoons rigani; serve with a squeeze of
lemon juice.

tips Don't overcook the calamari or it will toughen.
It should take about 30 seconds to cook one small
batch at a time. Reheat the oil before frying the next
batch of calamari. Ask your fishmonger to clean the
calamari for you.
serving suggestion Lemon wedges.

SPANAKOPITA

prep + cook time **50 minutes** makes **16**
nutritional count per triangle **11.1g total fat**
(6.4g saturated fat); 690kJ (165 cal);
11g carbohydrate; 4.7g protein; 1.5g fibre

1.5kg (3 pounds) silver beet
  (swiss chard), trimmed
1 tablespoon olive oil
1 medium brown onion (150g),
  chopped finely
2 cloves garlic, crushed
1 teaspoon ground nutmeg
200g (6½ ounces) fetta cheese, crumbled
1 tablespoon finely grated lemon rind
¼ cup each coarsely chopped fresh mint,
  flat-leaf parsley and dill
4 green onions (scallions), chopped finely
16 sheets fillo pastry
125g (4 ounces) butter, melted
2 teaspoons sesame seeds

1 Boil, steam or microwave silver beet until just wilted; drain. When cool enough to handle, squeeze excess liquid from silver beet; drain on absorbent paper. Chop silver beet coarsely; spread out on absorbent paper.
2 Heat oil in small frying pan; cook brown onion and garlic, stirring, until onion is soft. Add nutmeg; cook, stirring, until fragrant. Combine onion mixture and silver beet in large bowl with cheese, rind, herbs and green onion; season to taste.
3 Preheat oven to 180°C/350°F. Oil oven trays.
4 Brush 1 sheet of pastry with some of the butter; fold lengthways into thirds, brushing with butter between each fold. Place rounded tablespoon of silver beet mixture at one narrow edge of folded pastry sheet, leaving a border. Fold one corner of pastry diagonally over filling to form a large triangle. Continue folding to end of pastry sheet, retaining triangular shape. Repeat with remaining ingredients to make 16 triangles in total.
5 Place triangles, seam-side down, on trays. Brush with remaining butter; sprinkle with sesame seeds. Bake spanakopita about 15 minutes or until browned lightly.

tips Spanakopita comes from the Greek words *spanaki* (spinach) and *pitta* (pie). When working with the first sheet of pastry, cover remaining pastry with a sheet of baking paper then a damp tea towel to prevent it from drying out.

PAN-FRIED HALOUMI

prep + cook time **5 minutes (+ standing)** serves **4**
nutritional count per serving **17.7g total fat**
(7g saturated fat); 853kJ (204 cal);
0.9g carbohydrate; 10.7g protein; 0.1g fibre

Cut 200g (6½ ounces) haloumi cheese into
slices. Combine cheese with 2 tablespoons
olive oil and 2 teaspoons rigani in shallow
bowl; season with pepper. Stand 30 minutes.
Drain oil mixture from haloumi into large frying
pan; heat oil, cook cheese until browned lightly.
Serve immediately.

tip Fried haloumi needs to be eaten as soon as possible
after cooking — it becomes tough and rubbery as it
cools. It only takes a minute or so to fry, so it is best to
make this dish just before serving.

THYME AND GARLIC OLIVES

prep + cook time **15 minutes (+ standing)** serves **12**
nutritional count per serving **7.4g total fat**
(1g saturated fat); 295kJ (70 cal);
0.6g carbohydrate; 0.4g protein; 0.7g fibre

Sterilise jar and lid (see tips). Meanwhile,
using a vegetable peeler, peel rind thinly
from 1 medium lemon, avoiding white pith.
Combine rind, ½ cup olive oil, 2 bruised garlic
cloves, 3 sprigs fresh thyme and 1 fresh bay
leaf in medium saucepan over medium heat;
heat until warm and garlic begins to sizzle.
Add 2 cups rinsed and drained large kalamata
olives; cook over low heat 10 minutes. Spoon
hot olives into sterilised jar. Seal jar while hot.

tips To sterilise, place jar and lid in the dishwasher
on the hottest rinse cycle. Don't use detergent.
Alternatively, lay the jar and lid in a large pan, cover
completely with cold water and gradually bring to the
boil; boil for 20 minutes. Once sterilised, place jar and
lid on a clean tea towel to dry. Serve olives warm if you
like or store olives in refrigerator for up to one week.

DEEP-FRIED ZUCCHINI BALLS

prep + cook time **20 minutes (+ standing)** makes **16**
nutritional count per ball **3.3g total fat**
(1g saturated fat); 224kJ (54 cal);
4g carbohydrate; 2g protein; 0.5g fibre

Coarsely grate 2 medium zucchini, place in strainer; sprinkle with 2 teaspoons coarse cooking salt (kosher salt). Stand 10 minutes; squeeze excess moisture from zucchini. Combine zucchini with 1 finely chopped small brown onion, 75g (2½ ounces) crumbled fetta cheese, ½ cup plain (all-purpose) flour, 1 egg, 2 tablespoons finely chopped fresh mint and 1 tablespoon milk in large bowl; season. Heat vegetable oil in medium saucepan or wok; deep-fry tablespoons of mixture, in batches, until browned. Drain on absorbent paper.

serving suggestion **Yogurt for dipping.**

HERBED FETTA CHEESE

prep time **15 minutes (+ refrigeration)** makes **1¼ cups**
nutritional count per teaspoon **1.3g total fat**
(0.8g saturated fat); 60kJ (14 cal); 0g carbohydrate;
0.6g protein; 0g fibre

Oil 1¼-cup (310ml) dish; line with plastic wrap. Process 200g (6½ ounces) fetta cheese and 30g (1 ounce) softened unsalted butter until smooth. Transfer to medium bowl; stir in 2 tablespoons finely chopped fresh oregano, 1 tablespoon finely chopped fresh mint and 1 teaspoon finely grated lemon rind. Season with pepper. Press mixture firmly into dish. Cover; refrigerate 2 hours. Unmould cheese onto plate; drizzle with 2 teaspoons olive oil.

tip **Vary the herbs or add finely chopped olives.**
serving suggestion **Celery sticks and bread.**

EGGPLANT DIP

prep + cook time **25 minutes (+ cooling)** makes **2½ cups**
nutritional count per tablespoon **1.9g total fat**
(0.3g saturated fat); 84kJ (20 cal);
0.6g carbohydrate; 0.3g protein; 0.5g fibre

Pierce 2 medium eggplants all over with a fork.
Grill eggplants over low flame of gas cooker
or barbecue until charred and tender. When
eggplants are cool enough to handle, peel
away and discard skin. Coarsely chop eggplant
flesh; combine with ¼ cup olive oil in large
bowl. Stir in 2 tablespoons finely chopped fresh
flat-leaf parsley, ½ finely chopped small red
onion, 1 finely chopped medium ripe tomato
and 1 tablespoon lemon juice; season to taste.

tip There are many versions of this dish. Grilling the
eggplant over a flame gives it a smoky flavour. If you
find it too messy, you can also roast them in the oven or
in a covered barbecue.
serving suggestion **Pitta bread.**

SKORDALIA

prep + cook time **40 minutes** makes **3 cups**
nutritional count per tablespoon **3.3g total fat**
(0.6g saturated fat); 165kJ (39 cal);
2g carbohydrate; 0.5g protein; 0.3g fibre

Boil, steam or microwave 3 medium unpeeled
potatoes until tender; drain. Meanwhile, pound
3 garlic cloves and ½ teaspoon salt in a mortar
and pestle until smooth, or, chop the garlic and
salt together on a board and use the flat side of
the knife blade to press garlic into a paste.
When potatoes are cool enough to handle,
halve and spoon out flesh. Push flesh through
sieve into large bowl. Whisk in ½ cup olive oil,
¼ cup lemon juice and garlic mixture, then
½ cup milk. Season to taste.

tip We used russet burbank potatoes, also known as
idaho potatoes. You can use other floury varieties such
as sebago or coliban.
serving suggestion **Pitta bread and raw vegetable sticks.**

TZATZIKI

prep time **10 minutes (+ refrigeration)** makes **1¾ cups**
nutritional count per tablespoon **1.7g total fat**
(1.1g saturated fat); 125kJ (30 cal);
2.3g carbohydrate; 1.4g protein; 0.1g fibre

Place 500g (1 pound) yogurt onto large square
of double-thickness muslin. Tie ends of muslin
together; hang over large bowl, or place in a
sieve to drain. Refrigerate about 2 hours or
until yogurt is thick; discard liquid in bowl.
Meanwhile, peel, seed and coarsely grate
1 lebanese cucumber. Combine cucumber
and ½ teaspoon salt in small bowl; stand
20 minutes. Gently squeeze excess moisture
from cucumber. Combine yogurt and cucumber
with 1 crushed garlic clove, 1 tablespoon
lemon juice and 2 tablespoons finely chopped
fresh mint in small bowl; season to taste.

tips Muslin, a cotton cloth, is available in craft and
cookware shops. There are many variations of this
classic mezze — cucumber can be diced instead of
grated, you can use dill and parsley instead of mint.
It's a great side to most meat dishes.

TARAMASALATA

prep + cook time **25 minutes (+ cooling)** makes **1⅔ cups**
nutritional count per tablespoon **10.7g total fat**
(1.6g saturated fat); 472kJ (113 cal);
2.6g carbohydrate; 1.6g protein; 0.3g fibre

Boil, steam or microwave 1 coarsely chopped
large potato until tender; cool. Refrigerate until
cold. Finely grate ½ small white onion. Mash
potato and grated onion in small bowl with
90g (3 ounces) tarama, ¾ cup extra light olive
oil, ¼ cup white wine vinegar and 1 tablespoon
lemon juice until smooth.

tips Tarama is salt-cured carp or cod roe, available in
fish shops. This recipe uses mashed potato but there
are variations using bread soaked in water. The colour
of this dip can vary from beige to pink depending on the
roe (commercial taramasalata is often coloured pink).

CHICKEN, LEMON AND RICE SOUP

prep + cook time 45 minutes serves 4
nutritional count per serving 8.4g total fat
(2.3g saturated fat); 1099kJ (263 cal);
16.3g carbohydrate; 30.3g protein; 0.5g fibre

2 teaspoons olive oil
1 small brown onion (80g), chopped finely
1 litre (4 cups) chicken stock
400g (12½ ounces) chicken breast fillets,
    chopped coarsely
⅓ cup (65g) arborio rice
2 eggs
⅓ cup (80ml) lemon juice
2 tablespoons finely chopped fresh
    flat-leaf parsley

1 Heat oil in large saucepan; cook onion,
stirring, until softened. Add stock, chicken
and rice; bring to the boil. Reduce heat;
simmer, covered, about 20 minutes or until
rice is tender. Remove from heat.
2 Whisk eggs and juice in small bowl until
smooth. Gradually whisk ½ cup hot soup into
egg mixture, then stir warmed egg mixture
back into soup. Season to taste.
3 Serve bowls of soup sprinkled with parsley.

tips This soup is our take on the classic avgolemono
(which translates as egg and lemon). There are as many
variations of this soup as there are Greek families, but
the avgolemono mixture, added near the end of the
cooking time, is always the crowning glory. Arborio
rice is an excellent choice for this recipe due to its high
starch level, making for a deliciously creamy soup.

MUSSEL AND ORZO BROTH

prep + cook time 45 minutes serves 6
nutritional count per serving 11.5g total fat
(2.4g saturated fat); 1758kJ (420 cal);
41.4g carbohydrate; 27.2g protein; 3.7g fibre

½ teaspoon saffron threads
½ cup (125ml) aniseed-flavoured liqueur
4 spring onions (100g)
2 small fennel bulbs (400g)
2 tablespoons olive oil
4 cloves garlic, sliced thinly
2 fresh small red thai (serrano) chillies,
  sliced thinly
400g (12½ ounces) canned
  chopped tomatoes
1.5 litres (6 cups) fish stock or water
1 cup (220g) orzo pasta
1kg (2 pounds) mussels, cleaned
400g (12½ ounces) firm white fish fillets,
  chopped coarsely

1 Soak saffron in liqueur in small bowl for
15 minutes.
2 Meanwhile, cut green stems from onions;
slice onion stems thinly. Slice onions thinly
lengthways. Reserve fennel fronds; slice fennel
thinly lengthways. Heat oil in large heavy-based
saucepan; cook onion, fennel, garlic and chilli,
stirring, about 10 minutes or until onion softens.
Add undrained tomatoes, saffron mixture and
stock; bring to the boil.
3 Add pasta; bring to the boil. Reduce heat;
simmer, uncovered, stirring occasionally, until
pasta is almost tender. Add mussels and fish,
return to the boil; simmer, covered, about
5 minutes or until mussels have opened and
fish is cooked. Season to taste.
4 Stir in chopped fennel fronds and sliced
onion stems.

tips Pernod and ouzo are examples of aniseed-
flavoured liqueur. We used blue-eye in this recipe, but
any firm white fish fillet is fine. Orzo is a rice-shaped
pasta available from Greek delicatessens and specialty
food stores; if unavailable, use risoni.
serving suggestion Crusty bread.

WATERMELON AND HALOUMI SALAD

prep + cook time **25 minutes (+ cooling)** serves **4**
nutritional count per serving **11.3g total fat**
(5.5g saturated fat); 795kJ (190 cal);
10.9g carbohydrate; 10.8g protein; 1.8g fibre

400g (12½ ounces) watermelon flesh,
    sliced thinly
180g (5½ ounces) haloumi cheese,
    sliced thickly
½ cup (75g) seeded kalamata olives
½ cup loosely packed fresh mint leaves
pickled red onion dressing
1 small red onion (100g), sliced thinly
¼ cup (60ml) red wine vinegar
2 teaspoons caster (superfine) sugar

1 Make pickled red onion dressing.
2 Cut watermelon into wedges.
3 Cook cheese, in batches, on heated oiled grill plate (or grill or barbecue or grill pan) until browned. Remove from grill plate.
4 Arrange watermelon and cheese on platter, drizzle with dressing; sprinkle with olives and mint. Season to taste.
pickled red onion dressing Place onion in small heatproof bowl. Stir vinegar and sugar in small saucepan over medium heat until sugar dissolves; bring to the boil. Pour dressing over onion; cool.

tip You will need about 600g (1¼ pounds) watermelon (weighed with skin) for this recipe.

CABBAGE SALAD

prep time **10 minutes** serves **6**
nutritional count per serving **6.1g total fat**
(1g saturated fat); 262kJ (63 cal);
1.3g carbohydrate; 0.7g protein; 1g fibre

Finely shred 250g (8 ounces) green cabbage.
Thinly slice 4 trimmed red radishes. Combine
cabbage and radish in large bowl. Just before
serving, add combined 2 tablespoons olive oil,
1½ tablespoons lemon juice and 2 teaspoons
finely chopped fresh dill to bowl; toss gently to
combine. Season to taste.

tip **Use a mandolin or V-slicer if you have one, to finely**
shred the cabbage and slice the radishes.

SPINACH AND FETTA SALAD

prep time **20 minutes** serves **4**
nutritional count per serving **23.3g total fat**
(4.6g saturated fat); 1040kJ (248 cal);
2g carbohydrate; 7.2g protein; 3.4g fibre

Using a zester remove rind from 1 medium
lemon in long thin strips; place in small
heatproof bowl. Cover with boiling water; drain.
Repeat process (cover with boiling water; drain)
two more times. Remove remaining skin and
pith from lemon. Segment flesh over small
bowl to catch juice; coarsely chop flesh.
Add well-drained rind and flesh to bowl
with juice; add 1 tablespoon olive oil and
1 tablespoon rigani, season to taste. Combine
50g (1½ ounces) baby spinach leaves and
1 cup each loosely packed fresh mint and dill
leaves in medium bowl. Just before serving,
add 80g (2½ ounces) crumbled soft fetta
cheese, ½ cup roasted pine nuts and dressing;
toss gently to combine.

GREEK SALAD

prep time **20 minutes** serves **4**
nutritional count per serving **25.8g total fat**
(9.6g saturated fat); 1359kJ (325 cal);
10.8g carbohydrate; 11.5g protein; 3.2g fibre

Whisk ¼ cup olive oil, 1 tablespoon lemon
juice, 1 tablespoon white wine vinegar,
1 tablespoon finely chopped fresh oregano
and 1 crushed garlic clove in large bowl.
Cut 3 medium tomatoes into wedges; add to
bowl with 2 coarsely chopped lebanese
cucumbers, 200g (6½ ounces) coarsely
chopped fetta cheese, 1 thinly sliced small red
capsicum (bell pepper), 1 thinly sliced small red
onion and ½ cup seeded black olives. Toss to
combine; season to taste.

PICKLED ZUCCHINI SALAD

prep + cook time **15 minutes (+ cooling)** serves **4**
nutritional count per serving **4.9g total fat**
(0.7g saturated fat); 280kJ (67 cal);
4.2g carbohydrate; 1.1g protein; 1.8g fibre

Using a vegetable peeler, slice 4 medium
zucchini lengthways into ribbons. Combine
zucchini with ½ cup fresh dill sprigs and
1 tablespoon finely grated lemon rind in
medium heatproof bowl. Stir ¼ cup white
wine vinegar, 2 teaspoons caster (superfine)
sugar and 1 teaspoon sea salt in small
saucepan over medium heat until sugar
dissolves; bring to the boil. Remove from heat;
stir in 1 tablespoon olive oil. Season. Pour hot
liquid over zucchini mixture. Cool.

BARBECUED
VINE LEAF-WRAPPED SARDINES

prep + cook time 1 hour serves 4
nutritional count per serving 20g total fat
(3.9g saturated fat); 1686kJ (403 cal);
17g carbohydrate; 37.9g protein; 3.6g fibre

12 small whole sardines (500g), cleaned
1 medium lemon (140g), halved, sliced thinly
12 fresh bay leaves
12 small preserved vine leaves
1 tablespoon olive oil
garlic and lemon potatoes
2 tablespoons olive oil
600g (1¼ pounds) small potatoes,
    sliced thinly
1 medium lemon (140g)
4 cloves garlic, sliced thinly

1 Rinse cavities of sardines, pat dry. Season
cavities; top each sardine with a lemon slice
and a bay leaf. Wrap each sardine tightly in a
vine leaf to enclose lemon and bay leaf, leaving
heads and tails exposed. Brush sardines with oil.
2 Make garlic and lemon potatoes.
3 Meanwhile, cook sardines on heated oiled grill
plate (or grill or barbecue) until cooked through.
4 Serve with potatoes and lemon wedges.
garlic and lemon potatoes Heat oil in large
frying pan; cook potatoes, turning, about
15 minutes or until starting to soften and brown.
Remove rind from lemon using a zester, add to
potatoes with garlic; cook, stirring, until potatoes
and garlic are cooked through. Season to taste.

tip Preserved vine leaves are available in cryovac
packets from some delicatessens and Middle Eastern
food shops; they must be rinsed well and dried
before using.
serving suggestion Sliced tomato and white onion salad.

SEAFOOD

OVEN-BAKED FISH WITH TOMATO AND OLIVES

prep + cook time **40 minutes** serves **4**
nutritional count per serving **2.9g total fat**
(0.5g saturated fat); 253kJ (60 cal);
1.8g carbohydrate; 5.9g protein; 1.3g fibre

4 x 260g (8½-ounce) whole white fish
1 tablespoon olive oil
2 medium red onions (340g), sliced thinly
2 stalks celery (300g), trimmed, sliced thinly
4 cloves garlic, sliced thinly
400g (12½ ounces) cherry tomatoes
¾ cup (120g) seeded black olives
1 medium lemon (140g), halved, sliced thinly
¼ cup fresh rosemary sprigs
1 cup (250ml) dry white wine
½ cup coarsely chopped fresh
   flat-leaf parsley

1 Preheat oven to 200°C/400°F.
2 Remove heads from fish; clean fish.
3 Heat oil in medium flameproof baking dish; cook onion, celery and garlic, stirring, until browned lightly. Add tomatoes, olives, lemon and rosemary.
4 Season fish; place on vegetables. Pour wine over fish. Roast, uncovered, about 15 minutes or until fish is cooked through.
5 Serve fish sprinkled with parsley.

tips We used plate-sized leather jackets in this recipe, but any white fish would be fine. Ask your fishmonger to remove the heads and clean the fish for you.
serving suggestions Potato, pasta or rice salad.

PRAWN SOUVLAKIA WITH TOMATO AND FENNEL SAUCE

prep + cook time **35 minutes (+ refrigeration)** makes **8**
nutritional count per skewer **7.5g total fat**
(1.3g saturated fat); 702kJ (168 cal);
5.9g carbohydrate; 15.4g protein; 2g fibre

16 uncooked large prawns (shrimp) (1.1kg)
2 tablespoons olive oil
3 cloves garlic, crushed
2 teaspoons dried mint
1 teaspoon finely grated lemon rind
2 tablespoons lemon juice
tomato and fennel sauce
2 baby fennel (260g)
1 tablespoon olive oil
1 medium brown onion (150g),
   chopped finely
2 cloves garlic, chopped finely
3 medium ripe tomatoes (450g),
   chopped coarsely
¼ cup (60ml) aniseed-flavoured liqueur
1 cup coarsely chopped fresh mint

1 Shell and devein prawns, leaving tails intact.
Combine prawns in large bowl with remaining
ingredients. Cover; refrigerate 1 hour.
2 Make tomato and fennel sauce.
3 Thread prawns onto eight metal skewers;
reserve marinade. Cook prawns on heated
oiled grill plate (or grill or barbecue),
brushing with reserved marinade, until prawns
change colour.
4 Serve prawns with sauce.
tomato and fennel sauce Reserve fennel
fronds; finely chop fennel and fronds, separately.
Heat oil in medium saucepan; cook onion,
garlic and fennel, stirring, until softened. Add
tomato and liqueur; cook until heated through.
Just before serving, stir in fronds and mint;
season to taste.

tip Pernod and ouzo are examples of aniseed-flavoured
liqueur.
serving suggestion Rice pilaf.

TUNA SOUVLAKIA WITH CHAR-GRILLED CAPSICUM SALAD

prep + cook time **40 minutes (+ refrigeration & cooling)**
serves **4** nutritional count per serving **9g total fat**
(1.4g saturated fat); 1155kJ (275 cal);
8.9g carbohydrate; 39.1g protein; 5.4g fibre

600g (1¼-pound) piece tuna
1½ tablespoons olive oil
1 tablespoon rigani
1 teaspoon dried chilli flakes
char-grilled capsicum salad
3 medium red capsicums
   (bell peppers) (600g)
3 medium yellow capsicums
   (bell peppers) (600g)
3 cloves garlic, sliced thinly
¾ cup loosely packed fresh oregano leaves
2 tablespoons red wine vinegar

1 Cut tuna into 3cm (1¼-inch) pieces. Combine tuna, oil, rigani and chilli in medium bowl; season. Thread tuna onto eight metal skewers; place in shallow dish, cover; refrigerate 30 minutes.

2 Meanwhile, make char-grilled capsicum salad.

3 Cook tuna on heated grill plate (or grill or barbecue) until cooked as desired.

4 Serve tuna with salad.

char-grilled capsicum salad Cook capsicums on heated grill plate (or grill or barbecue) over high heat, turning, until skin blisters and blackens. Place capsicums in large bowl, cover with plastic; cool. Peel away skin, then slice capsicum thinly. Combine capsicum in medium bowl with garlic, oregano and vinegar; season to taste.

RABBIT STIFADO

prep + cook time 2 hours 35 minutes (+ refrigeration)
serves 4 nutritional count per serving 27.9g total fat
(5.7g saturated fat); 2284kJ (546 cal);
12.8g carbohydrate; 54.3g protein; 4.6g fibre

1.4kg (2¾-pound) whole rabbit
⅔ cup (160ml) dry red wine
⅓ cup (80ml) red wine vinegar
2 cloves garlic, crushed
3 dried bay leaves
1 cinnamon stick
6 cloves
1 tablespoon light brown sugar
2 teaspoons rigani
½ teaspoon ground allspice
800g (1½ pounds) baby brown onions
¼ cup (60ml) olive oil
2 tablespoons tomato paste
1 litre (4 cups) water
2 tablespoons coarsely chopped
   fresh flat-leaf parsley

1 Chop rabbit into eight even-sized pieces.
Combine rabbit, wine, vinegar, garlic, bay
leaves, cinnamon, cloves, sugar, rigani and
allspice in large bowl. Cover; refrigerate 3 hours
or overnight.
2 Peel onions, leaving root ends intact. Heat
oil in large saucepan; cook onions, stirring,
over medium heat, until softened. Remove
from pan.
3 Remove rabbit from marinade; reserve
marinade. Cook rabbit in same heated pan,
in batches, until browned. Remove from pan.
4 Return rabbit and onions to pan with paste,
the water and reserved marinade; bring to the
boil. Reduce heat; simmer, uncovered, over low
heat, about 2 hours or until sauce has thickened.
Season to taste. Serve topped with parsley.

tip Ask the butcher to chop the rabbit into pieces for you.
serving suggestion Crusty bread.

ROASTED GARLIC, LEMON AND OREGANO CHICKEN

prep + cook time **1 hour 40 minutes** serves **4**
nutritional count per serving **46.2g total fat**
(9.8g saturated fat); 3793kJ (906 cal);
48.1g carbohydrate; 73.5g protein; 7.3g fibre

1.5kg (3 pounds) medium potatoes,
  quartered lengthways
4 chicken marylands (1.4kg)
½ cup (125ml) lemon juice
½ cup (125ml) olive oil
6 cloves garlic, chopped finely
2 teaspoons rigani
1½ cups (375ml) water

1 Preheat oven to 180°C/350°F.
2 Place potatoes in large baking dish; top with chicken. Combine juice, oil, garlic and rigani in small jug; pour over chicken and potatoes, then add the water. Season.
3 Roast chicken and potatoes, uncovered, about 1½ hours or until chicken is tender and browned.

GRILLED LEMON CHICKEN

prep + cook time **30 minutes** serves **8**
nutritional count per serving **30g total fat**
(7g saturated fat); 1690kJ (404 cal);
1g carbohydrate; 33g protein; 0.1g fibre

½ cup (125ml) olive oil
½ cup (125ml) lemon juice
1.5kg (3 pounds) chicken thigh fillets
2 teaspoons rigani
2 teaspoons coarse cooking salt
   (kosher salt)
1 teaspoon ground white pepper
1 medium lemon (140g), cut into wedges

1 Blend or process oil and juice until thick and creamy.
2 Combine chicken, rigani, salt, pepper and half the lemon mixture in medium bowl. Thread chicken onto eight oiled metal skewers.
3 Cook skewers on heated oiled grill plate (or grill or barbecue), brushing frequently with remaining lemon mixture until cooked through.
4 Serve skewers with lemon wedges.

serving suggestion **Green salad.**

MOUSSAKA

prep + cook time 1 hour 50 minutes serves 6
nutritional count per serving 36.6g total fat
(16.5g saturated fat); 2420kJ (579 cal);
18g carbohydrate; 41.8g protein; 5.3g fibre

¼ cup (60ml) olive oil
2 large eggplants (1kg), sliced thinly
1 large brown onion (200g), chopped finely
2 cloves garlic, crushed
1kg (2 pounds) minced (ground) lamb
400g (12½ ounces) canned
    crushed tomatoes
½ cup (125ml) dry white wine
1 teaspoon ground cinnamon
¼ cup (20g) finely grated kefalotyri cheese
white sauce
75g (2½ ounces) butter
⅓ cup (50g) plain (all-purpose) flour
2 cups (500ml) milk

1 Heat oil in large frying pan; cook eggplant,
in batches, until browned both sides. Drain on
absorbent paper.
2 Cook onion and garlic in same pan, stirring,
until onion softens. Add lamb; cook, stirring,
until browned. Stir in undrained tomatoes, wine
and cinnamon; bring to the boil. Reduce heat;
simmer, uncovered, about 30 minutes or until
liquid has evaporated. Season to taste.
3 Meanwhile, preheat oven to 180°C/350°F.
Oil shallow 2-litre (8-cup) rectangular baking dish.
4 Make white sauce.
5 Place one-third of the eggplant, overlapping
slices slightly, in dish; spread half the meat
sauce over eggplant. Repeat layering with
another third of the eggplant, remaining meat
sauce and remaining eggplant. Spread white
sauce over top layer of eggplant; sprinkle
with cheese.
6 Bake moussaka about 40 minutes or until
top browns lightly. Cover; stand 10 minutes
before serving.
white sauce Melt butter in medium saucepan,
add flour; cook, stirring, until mixture bubbles
and thickens. Gradually add milk; stir until
mixture boils and thickens.

serving suggestion Green salad.

PASTITSIO

prep + cook time **2 hours 15 minutes** serves **6**
nutritional count per serving **45.8g total fat**
(23.2g saturated fat); 3440kJ (823 cal);
51.6g carbohydrate; 48.4g protein; 4g fibre

250g (8 ounces) macaroni pasta
2 eggs, beaten lightly
¾ cup (60g) coarsely grated kefalotyri cheese
2 tablespoons stale breadcrumbs
meat sauce
2 tablespoons olive oil
2 medium brown onions (300g),
  chopped finely
750g (1½ pounds) minced (ground) lamb
400g (12½ ounces) canned crushed tomatoes
⅓ cup (90g) tomato paste
½ cup (125ml) beef stock
¼ cup (60ml) dry white wine
½ teaspoon ground cinnamon
1 egg, beaten lightly
cheese sauce
90g (3 ounces) butter
½ cup (75g) plain (all-purpose) flour
3½ cups (875ml) milk
1 cup (80g) coarsely grated kefalotyri cheese
2 egg yolks

1 Preheat oven to 180°C/350°F. Oil shallow 2.5-litre (10-cup) ovenproof dish.
2 Make meat sauce and cheese sauce.
3 Cook pasta in large saucepan of boiling water until tender; drain. Combine hot pasta, egg and cheese in large bowl. Press pasta over base of dish.
4 Top pasta evenly with meat sauce; pour over cheese sauce. Smooth surface; sprinkle with breadcrumbs.
5 Bake pastitsio about 1 hour or until browned lightly. Stand 10 minutes before serving.
meat sauce Heat oil in large saucepan; cook onion and lamb, stirring, until lamb is browned. Stir in undrained tomatoes, paste, stock, wine and cinnamon; simmer, uncovered, about 20 minutes or until mixture is thick. Season to taste. Cool; stir in egg.
cheese sauce Melt butter in medium saucepan, add flour; cook, stirring, until mixture bubbles and thickens. Remove from heat; gradually add milk. Stir over heat until sauce boils and thickens; stir in cheese. Cool 5 minutes; stir in egg yolks.

SLOW-ROASTED LAMB WITH SKORDALIA AND POTATOES

prep + cook time **4 hours (+ refrigeration)** serves **4**
nutritional count per serving **57g total fat**
(14g saturated fat); 4556kJ (1090 cal);
51.5g carbohydrate; 91.2g protein; 6.7g fibre

2kg (4-pound) leg of lamb
2 cloves garlic, crushed
½ cup (125ml) lemon juice
2 tablespoons olive oil
1 tablespoon fresh oregano leaves
2 teaspoons fresh lemon thyme leaves
5 large potatoes (1.5kg), chopped coarsely
1 tablespoon finely grated lemon rind
2 tablespoons lemon juice, extra
2 tablespoons olive oil, extra
skordalia
1 medium potato (200g), quartered
3 cloves garlic, crushed
1 tablespoon lemon juice
1 tablespoon white wine vinegar
2 tablespoons water
⅓ cup (80ml) olive oil

1 Combine lamb, garlic, juice, oil, oregano and half the thyme in large bowl. Cover; refrigerate 3 hours or overnight.
2 Preheat oven to 160°C/325°F.
3 Place lamb mixture in large baking dish; roast, uncovered, 3 hours.
4 Meanwhile, make skordalia.
5 Combine potatoes, rind, extra juice, extra oil and remaining thyme in large bowl; season. Place potatoes, in single layer, on oven tray. Roast potatoes, uncovered, for last 30 minutes of lamb cooking time.
6 Remove lamb from oven; cover to keep warm.
7 Increase oven to 220°C/425°F; roast potatoes a further 20 minutes or until browned lightly and cooked through.
8 Serve potatoes and lamb with skordalia and pan juices.
skordalia Boil, steam or microwave potato until tender; drain. Push potato through fine sieve into medium bowl; cool 10 minutes. Whisk combined garlic, juice, vinegar and the water into potato. Gradually whisk in oil in a thin, steady stream; continue whisking until skordalia thickens. Stir in about a tablespoon of warm water if skordalia becomes too thick.

LEMON AND GARLIC LAMB KEBABS

prep + cook time **30 minutes** serves **4**
nutritional count per serving **15.9g total fat**
(4.3g saturated fat); 1250kJ (299 cal);
0.4g carbohydrate; 38.6g protein; 0.4g fibre

8 x 15cm (6-inch) stalks fresh rosemary
750g (1½ pounds) lamb fillets, cut into
   3cm (1¼-inch) pieces
3 cloves garlic, crushed
2 tablespoons olive oil
2 teaspoons finely grated lemon rind
1 tablespoon lemon juice

1 Remove leaves from bottom two-thirds of each rosemary stalk; sharpen trimmed ends to a point.
2 Thread lamb onto rosemary skewers. Brush kebabs with combined garlic, oil, rind and juice. Cover; refrigerate until required.
3 Cook kebabs on heated oiled grill plate (or grill or barbecue), brushing frequently with remaining garlic mixture, until cooked.
4 Serve kebabs with a greek salad, if you like.

BAKED LAMB SHANKS WITH ORZO

prep + cook time 2 hours 10 minutes serves 4
nutritional count per serving 14g total fat
(4.2g saturated fat); 2045kJ (488 cal);
53.8g carbohydrate; 35.9g protein; 4.6g fibre

1 tablespoon olive oil
4 french-trimmed lamb shanks (1kg)
1 medium brown onion (150g),
   chopped finely
3 cinnamon sticks
1 dried bay leaf
3 cloves garlic, crushed
400g (12½ ounces) canned diced tomatoes
2 cups (500ml) chicken stock
1¼ cups (275g) orzo pasta
1 cup (250ml) water
2 tablespoons fresh oregano leaves

1 Preheat oven to 200°C/400°F.
2 Heat oil in large baking dish; cook lamb over medium heat until browned all over. Remove from dish.
3 Cook onion, cinnamon and bay leaf in same dish, stirring, until onion softens. Add garlic; cook, stirring, until fragrant. Return lamb to dish with undrained tomatoes and stock; bring to the boil. Cover dish with lid or foil; cook in oven 1¼ hours.
4 Stir pasta and the water into dish; cook, covered, about 30 minutes or until lamb and pasta are tender. Season to taste.
5 Serve lamb sprinkled with oregano.

tips You can replace orzo with risoni if you like. Orzo, like risoni, absorbs cooking liquid. If the sauce is too thick, stir in a little extra water. If you make this dish in advance, you will need to add some water or stock when reheating.

GOAT AND CAPSICUM STEW

prep + cook time **3 hours 15 minutes** serves **6**
nutritional count per serving **17.5g total fat**
(4.1g saturated fat); 2105kJ (503 cal);
6.9g carbohydrate; 74.5g protein; 3.3g fibre

¼ cup (60ml) olive oil
1.6kg (3¼-pound) boneless goat shoulder,
    chopped coarsely
2 medium brown onions (300g), sliced thinly
1 dried bay leaf
400g (12½ ounces) canned diced tomatoes
½ cup (125ml) chicken stock
2 teaspoons rigani
2 medium red capsicums (bell peppers)
    (400g), sliced thinly
1 medium yellow capsicum (bell pepper)
    (200g), sliced thinly
2 tablespoons coarsely chopped fresh
    flat-leaf parsley

1 Heat 2 tablespoons of the oil in large saucepan; cook goat, in batches, until browned. Remove from pan.
2 Heat remaining oil in same pan; cook onion and bay leaf, stirring, until onion softens.
Return goat to pan with undrained tomatoes, stock and rigani; bring to the boil. Reduce heat; simmer, covered, 2½ hours.
3 Stir in capsicum; simmer, covered, about 20 minutes or until capsicum is tender.
Season to taste. Serve sprinkled with parsley.

tip Goat shoulder is good for stews and casseroles as it needs long slow cooking to be tender. It is sold in Greek and specialty butchers and often comes frozen. Ask the butcher to cut the meat into chunks while frozen and thaw meat in refrigerator at home.
serving suggestions Rice or mashed potatoes.

BARBECUED LAMB SANDWICHES

prep + cook time **1 hour (+ refrigeration & standing)**
serves **6** nutritional count per serving **18.8g total fat**
(5.5g saturated fat); 2064kJ (493 cal);
44.8g carbohydrate; 36.3g protein; 4.9g fibre

1 medium lemon (140g)
900g (1¾-pound) boneless lamb shoulder
3 cloves garlic, crushed
2 tablespoons fresh oregano leaves
2 sprigs fresh thyme
2 tablespoons olive oil
¼ medium iceberg lettuce, shredded finely
2 medium tomatoes (300g), sliced thinly
1 small red onion (100g), sliced thinly
1 cup (140g) tzatziki
6 large pitta breads (480g), toasted lightly

1 Using a vegetable peeler, peel rind thinly from lemon, avoiding white pith. Combine lamb, rind, garlic, herbs and oil in shallow dish, cover; refrigerate 4 hours. Drain lamb; season.
2 Heat grill plate (or grill or barbecue); cook lamb, covered, about 25 minutes, turning halfway through. Stand lamb, loosely covered with foil, 15 minutes before slicing.
3 Serve lamb with lettuce, tomato, onion and tzatziki on warmed pitta bread.

tips This is a homemade version of the Greek sandwich, called gyros. Gyros are made from slices of meat cooked on a turning spit. You can make your own tzatziki (page 17) for this recipe, if you like.

BRAISED GREEN BEANS

prep + cook time 45 minutes **serves** 6
nutritional count per serving 3.5g total fat
(0.5g saturated fat); 443kJ (106 cal);
11.8g carbohydrate; 4.1g protein; 4.7g fibre

4 silver beet (swiss chard) leaves (350g)
1 tablespoon olive oil
1 small brown onion (80g), sliced thinly
2 cloves garlic, sliced thinly
1 fresh small red thai (serrano) chilli,
　sliced thinly
8 baby new potatoes (320g), quartered
400g (12½ ounces) canned
　chopped tomatoes
300g (9½ ounces) baby green beans, trimmed

1 Wash and dry silver beet; finely chop leaves
and stems, separately.
2 Heat oil in medium heavy-based saucepan;
cook silver beet stems, onion, garlic and chilli,
stirring, about 10 minutes or until stems soften.
3 Add potato and undrained tomatoes;
simmer, covered, 15 minutes. Add beans;
cook, uncovered, about 5 minutes or until
potato is tender. Season to taste.
4 Just before serving, add silver beet leaves;
cook about 3 minutes or until wilted.

SLOW-COOKED POTATOES WITH WINE AND HERBS

prep + cook time **55 minutes** serves **4**
nutritional count per serving **11g total fat**
(3.6g saturated fat); 970kJ (232 cal);
22.8g carbohydrate; 8g protein; 5.3g fibre

1 medium lemon (140g)
600g (1¼ pounds) kipfler (fingerling)
  potatoes, halved lengthways
1 tablespoon olive oil
1 medium brown onion (150g), sliced thinly
12 unpeeled garlic cloves
1 tablespoon rigani
4 dried bay leaves
½ cup (125ml) dry white wine
1 cup (250ml) chicken stock
⅓ cup (50g) seeded kalamata olives
⅓ cup (65g) fetta cheese, crumbled

1 Preheat oven to 160°C/325°F.
2 Finely grate rind from the lemon. Squeeze
lemon; you need ¼ cup juice. Combine
potatoes and juice in large bowl; season.
3 Heat oil in medium baking dish; cook onion
and garlic, stirring, until onion softens. Add
potatoes with juice, rigani, rind and bay leaves;
stir to coat in onion mixture. Add wine and
stock; bring to the boil.
4 Roast potato mixture, uncovered, in oven,
stirring occasionally, about 40 minutes or until
potatoes are tender.
5 Serve potatoes with olives and cheese.

BROAD BEANS AND ARTICHOKES

prep + cook time **20 minutes** serves **4**
nutritional count per serving **9.5g total fat**
(1.5g saturated fat); 539kJ (129 cal);
4.4g carbohydrate; 6.1g protein; 10.6g fibre

300g (9½ ounces) fresh or frozen broad
(fava) beans
400g (12½ ounces) canned artichoke hearts,
drained, halved
tomato dressing
1 medium tomato (150g), seeded,
chopped finely
2 tablespoons finely shredded fresh basil
2 tablespoons olive oil
1 tablespoon white wine vinegar

1 Make tomato dressing.
2 Add shelled broad beans to saucepan of
boiling salted water, boil, uncovered, about
2 minutes or until skins wrinkle; drain. Transfer
to bowl of iced water, stand 2 minutes; drain.
Peel broad beans; discard skins.
3 Place beans in medium bowl with artichokes
and dressing; toss gently to combine. Season
to taste.
tomato dressing Combine ingredients in
small bowl.

tip You will need about 1.25kg (2½ pounds) fresh broad
beans for this recipe.

HALVA

prep + cook time 30 minutes (+ standing) **serves** 20
nutritional count per serving 12.4g total fat
(6g saturated fat); 1097kJ (262 cal);
36g carbohydrate; 3g protein; 1.3g fibre

2 cups (440g) caster (superfine) sugar
1 litre (4 cups) water
2 whole cloves
1 cinnamon stick
220g (7 ounces) butter, chopped coarsely
2 cups (320g) semolina
½ cup (80g) coarsely chopped
   blanched almonds
2 teaspoons finely grated orange rind
½ cup (80g) coarsely chopped raisins
¼ cup (40g) blanched whole almonds, roasted
1 teaspoon ground cinnamon

1 Grease 20cm x 30cm (8-inch x 12-inch)
slice pan or ovenproof dish; line base with
baking paper, extending paper 5cm (2 inches)
over short sides.
2 Stir sugar, the water, cloves and cinnamon
stick in medium saucepan over heat until sugar
dissolves. Bring to the boil; boil, uncovered,
without stirring, 5 minutes. Cool 5 minutes.
3 Meanwhile, heat butter in large saucepan
until foaming. Add semolina and chopped
nuts; cook, stirring, about 8 minutes or until
browned lightly. Remove from heat. Carefully
strain sugar syrup into semolina mixture
(mixture will bubble up).
4 Return pan to heat, add rind and raisins;
cook, stirring, about 1 minute or until thick and
starting to come away from the side of the pan.
5 Spread semolina mixture into pan; top with
whole nuts, cool. Sprinkle with sifted ground
cinnamon before cutting.

SWEETS

BAKLAVA

prep + cook time **1 hour 20 minutes (+ cooling)** makes **30**
nutritional count per piece **16.4g total fat
(6.1g saturated fat); 1010kJ (240 cal);
21g carbohydrate; 3.6g protein; 1.4g fibre**

1½ cups (200g) shelled unsalted
   pistachio nuts
2 cups (200g) walnut pieces
¼ cup (55g) caster (superfine) sugar
2 tablespoons fine semolina
1 teaspoon ground cinnamon
pinch ground cloves
375g (12 ounces) fillo pastry
310g (10 ounces) butter, melted
30 whole cloves
syrup
1 cup (220g) caster (superfine) sugar
1 cup (250ml) water
¼ cup (90g) honey
1 tablespoon lemon juice
1 cinnamon stick

1 Preheat oven to 200°C/400°F. Grease
20cm x 30cm (8-inch x 12-inch) lamington pan.
2 Process nuts, sugar, semolina, cinnamon
and ground cloves until chopped finely; transfer
to medium bowl.
3 Brush 1 sheet of pastry with a little of the
butter; top with 7 more sheets, brushing each
well with butter. Fold pastry in half, place into
pan. Sprinkle pastry with thin even layer of the
nut mixture. Layer another 2 sheets of pastry,
brushing each well with more butter. Fold
pastry in half, place in pan; top with another
layer of nut mixture. Repeat layering process
until all nut mixture has been used. Repeat
layering and buttering with remaining pastry
sheets; fold in half, place on top of nuts, brush
with butter. Score the top lightly in diamond
pattern; press one whole clove into centre of
each piece.
4 Bake baklava about 50 minutes.
5 Meanwhile, make syrup.
6 Pour syrup over hot baklava. Cool
before cutting.
syrup Stir ingredients in small saucepan
over heat until sugar dissolves; bring to the
boil. Reduce heat; simmer, uncovered, about
10 minutes or until thickened slightly. Discard
cinnamon; cool syrup.

ALMOND AND WALNUT PASTRIES (KATAIFI)

prep + cook time 55 minutes (+ cooling) makes 18
nutritional count per piece 19.1g total fat
(8.1g saturated fat); 1500kJ (358 cal);
43.6g carbohydrate; 4.9g protein; 1.6g fibre

1 cup (160g) almond kernels, chopped finely
½ cup (50g) walnut pieces, chopped finely
½ cup (35g) stale breadcrumbs
2 teaspoons caster (superfine) sugar
1 teaspoon ground cinnamon
1 egg
375g (12 ounce) kataifi pastry
250g (8 ounces) unsalted butter, melted
lemon syrup
2 cups (440g) caster (superfine) sugar
1 cup (250ml) water
¼ cup (90g) honey
4 x 5cm (2-inch) strips lemon rind
2 tablespoons lemon juice

1 Preheat oven to 200°C/400°F. Grease
20cm x 30cm (8-inch x 12-inch) lamington pan.
2 Combine nuts, breadcrumbs, sugar,
cinnamon and egg in medium bowl.
3 Lightly pull the pastry apart. Spread ½ cup
of pastry into 5cm x 20cm (2-inch x 8-inch)
rectangular shape; brush with some of the
butter. Place 1 level tablespoon of the nut
mixture along one short side of the pastry; roll
up tightly, place seam-side down in pan.
Repeat with remaining pastry, butter and nut
mixture.
4 Bake pastries about 35 minutes.
5 Meanwhile, make lemon syrup.
6 Pour hot syrup over hot pastries in pan. Cool.
lemon syrup Stir ingredients in small saucepan
over heat until sugar dissolves; bring to the boil.
Reduce heat; simmer, uncovered, about 10
minutes or until thickened slightly. Discard rind.

tips Kataifi is finely shredded fillo pastry available from
Middle Eastern grocery stores. During preparation, keep
the pastry covered with baking paper then a damp
tea-towel to prevent the pastry drying out.

GREEK COFFEE

prep + cook time **10 minutes** serves **4**
nutritional count per serving **0g total fat**
(0g saturated fat); 107kJ (26 cal);
6g carbohydrate; 0.6g protein; 0.7g fibre

Place 1 cup cold water in 4 demitasse-cup
capacity briki or small saucepan. Add
1½ tablespoons ground greek coffee and
3 teaspoons caster (superfine) sugar; stir over
low heat until sugar dissolves. Slowly bring to
the boil; remove from heat when froth almost
reaches the top of briki. Divide froth among
4 demitasse cups, then carefully fill the cups
with remaining coffee mixture. Serve coffee
immediately with a glass of cold water.

tips A traditional briki (small pot) is the best pot to use
when making Greek coffee because it allows the proper
amount of froth to form, which in turn adds to the unique
taste. Brikis are available from Greek and Middle Eastern
delicatessens. A demitasse cup holds about ¼ cup (60ml).

FIG GALETTES

prep + cook time **30 minutes** makes **4**
nutritional count per galette **21.4g total fat**
(5.1g saturated fat); 1446kJ (346 cal);
32.2g carbohydrate; 5.5g protein; 3.4g fibre

Preheat oven to 180°C/350°F. Line oven tray
with baking paper. Cut four 12cm (4¾-inch)
rounds from 1 sheet puff pastry; sprinkle with
⅓ cup ground almonds. Thinly slice 4 large
fresh figs, place on top of rounds; brush with
combined 30g (1 ounce) melted butter and
2 tablespoons pure maple syrup. Turn edges
of pastry up. Bake galettes about 20 minutes
or until pastry is puffed and golden. Serve
warm, dusted with 2 teaspoons sifted icing
(confectioners') sugar.

SPICED PLUMS WITH YOGURT

prep + cook time **15 minutes (+ standing)** serves **6**
nutritional count per serving **3.4g total fat**
(2.1g saturated fat); 543kJ (130 cal);
21.5g carbohydrate; 3g protein; 0.9g fibre

Drain juice from 1.6kg (3¼ pounds) canned
whole plums into medium saucepan; reserve
plums. Add 2 cinnamon sticks and 6 cardamom
pods; bring to the boil. Reduce heat; simmer,
uncovered, 3 minutes. Remove pan from heat.
Add plums; cover pan, stand 10 minutes.
Serve warm plums with 1 cup yogurt; drizzle
with juice mixture.

tip **You will need 2 x 825g (1¾-pound) cans whole**
plums for this recipe.

ALMOND BISCUITS

prep + cook time **45 minutes (+ cooling)** makes **25**
nutritional count per biscuit **9g total fat**
(0.6g saturated fat); 568kJ (136 cal);
9.5g carbohydrate; 3.7g protein; 1.4g fibre

Preheat oven to 180°C/350°F. Line oven trays
with baking paper. Combine 3 cups ground
almonds, 1 cup caster (superfine) sugar and
3 drops almond essence in large bowl. Add
3 lightly beaten egg whites; stir until mixture
forms a firm paste. Place 1 cup flaked almonds
in small shallow bowl. Roll level tablespoons of
paste mixture in nuts; roll into 8cm (3¼-inch)
logs. Press on remaining almonds. Shape logs
to form crescents; place on trays. Bake biscuits
about 15 minutes or until browned lightly; cool
on trays.

GALAKTOBOUREKO

prep + cook time 1 hour 40 minutes (+ cooling)
makes 21 nutritional count per piece 9.8g total fat
(5.9g saturated fat); 1182kJ (282 cal);
44.9g carbohydrate; 5.2g protein; 0.5g fibre

1.25 litres (5 cups) milk
1¾ cups (385g) caster (superfine) sugar
1 vanilla bean, split lengthways
1 cup (160g) fine semolina
20g (¾ ounce) butter
4 eggs
16 sheets fillo pastry
150g (5 ounces) butter, melted
1 tablespoon icing (confectioners') sugar
¼ teaspoon ground cinnamon
lemon syrup
1 cup (220g) caster (superfine) sugar
¾ cup (180ml) water
2 x 5cm (2-inch) strips lemon rind
2 teaspoons lemon juice

1 Stir milk, sugar and vanilla bean in large saucepan over heat until sugar dissolves; bring to the boil. Gradually whisk semolina into milk mixture; whisk over medium heat about 5 minutes or until thickened.

2 Remove pan from heat; discard vanilla bean. Stir in butter. Transfer custard to large heatproof bowl; cover surface of custard with plastic wrap. Cool 1 hour. Stir in eggs.

3 Preheat oven to 160°C/325°F. Grease deep 25cm x 32cm (10-inch x 13-inch) baking dish.

4 Cut pastry sheets to the same size as dish; discard excess pastry. Brush 1 sheet of pastry with some of the butter; top with 7 more pastry sheets, brushing each with butter. Place in base of dish; spread custard into dish. Repeat with remaining pastry and butter; place on top of custard.

5 Bake galaktoboureko about 55 minutes or until custard is set.

6 Meanwhile, make lemon syrup.

7 Pour hot syrup over hot galaktoboureko; cool. Serve dusted with combined sifted icing sugar and cinnamon.

lemon syrup Stir ingredients in small saucepan over heat until sugar dissolves; bring to the boil. Reduce heat; simmer, uncovered, about 10 minutes or until thickened slightly. Discard rind.

CHERRY SPOON SWEET

prep + cook time **15 minutes (+ cooling)** serves **6**
nutritional count per serving **0.1g total fat**
(0g saturated fat); 800kJ (191 cal);
48.7g carbohydrate; 0.6g protein; 0.7g fibre

Drain 425g (13½ ounces) canned seedless
black cherries in syrup over small saucepan;
reserve cherries. Add 1 cup caster (superfine)
sugar, 1 split vanilla bean, 2 x 5cm (2-inch)
strips lemon rind and 1 teaspoon lemon juice
to pan; stir over heat until sugar dissolves.
Add reserved cherries, bring to the boil; boil,
uncovered, about 7 minutes or until mixture
thickens and will coat the back of a metal
spoon. Cool to room temperature.

serving suggestion **This is traditionally served with a
glass of cold water when guests arrive.**

ORANGE SPOON SWEET

prep + cook time **1 hour (+ standing & cooling)** serves **12**
nutritional count per serving **0g total fat**
(0g saturated fat); 588kJ (140 cal);
36.7g carbohydrate; 0g protein; 0.2g fibre

Using a vegetable peeler, remove and discard
the rind from 3 medium oranges. Trim the ends
from the oranges to expose the orange flesh.
Cut each orange into 8 wedges; cut the white
pith away from the flesh. Reserve flesh for
another use. Cut strips of pith in half diagonally.
Place pith in medium saucepan with enough
cold water to cover completely. Bring to the
boil; boil, uncovered, 5 minutes. Drain, rinse
pith under cold water. Repeat process two
more times. Dry pith on absorbent paper for
30 minutes. Stir 2 cups caster (superfine) sugar
and 1¼ cups water in small saucepan over
heat until sugar dissolves. Add pith; bring to
the boil. Boil, uncovered, about 10 minutes or
until mixture thickens enough to coat the back
of a metal spoon. Stir in 1 teaspoon lemon
juice. Cool to room temperature.

CARAMELISED FIGS & YOGURT

prep + cook time **20 minutes** serves **4**
nutritional count per serving **6g total fat**
(1.3g saturated fat); 777kJ (186 cal);
26.1g carbohydrate; 6.8g protein; 3.6g fibre

Combine 1 cup low-fat yogurt, ¼ cup coarsely
chopped roasted unsalted pistachio nuts,
¼ teaspoon ground nutmeg and 1 tablespoon
caster (superfine) sugar in small bowl. Halve
6 large fresh figs lengthways. Brush cut-side
of figs with 1 tablespoon honey. Cook figs,
cut-side down, in heated large non-stick
frying pan 5 minutes. Turn figs; cook, about
5 minutes or until browned. Serve figs with
spiced yogurt.

YOGURT CAKE

prep + cook time **1 hour (+ cooling)** serves **12**
nutritional count per serving **12.8g total fat**
(6.7g saturated fat); 1216kJ (291 cal);
37.3g carbohydrate; 5.9g protein; 1.2g fibre

Preheat oven to 180°C/350°F. Grease
20cm x 30cm (8-inch x 12-inch) lamington
pan; line base and sides with baking paper.
Separate 3 eggs. Beat 125g (4 ounces)
softened butter and 1 cup caster (superfine)
sugar in small bowl with electric mixer until light
and fluffy. Beat in egg yolks. Transfer mixture to
large bowl; stir in sifted 2 cups self-raising flour
and ½ teaspoon bicarbonate of soda (baking
soda), in two batches. Stir in ¼ cup finely
chopped blanched almonds and 1 cup yogurt.
Beat egg whites in clean small bowl with
electric mixer until soft peaks form. Fold egg
whites into yogurt mixture, in two batches.
Spread mixture into pan. Bake cake about
35 minutes. Turn cake onto wire rack to cool.

serving suggestion **Dusted icing (confectioners') sugar.**

MILOPITA

prep + cook time **1 hour 30 minutes** serves **8**
nutritional count per serving **22.5g total fat**
(14.2g saturated fat); 1962kJ (470 cal);
61.1g carbohydrate; 6.2g protein; 1.8g fibre

3 medium apples (450g), peeled,
  cored, quartered
¼ cup (60ml) lemon juice
60g (2 ounces) butter
¼ cup (55g) firmly packed light brown sugar
1 teaspoon ground cinnamon
125g (4 ounces) butter, softened, extra
1 cup (220g) caster (superfine) sugar
1 tablespoon finely grated lemon rind
1 teaspoon vanilla extract
2 eggs, separated
1 cup (150g) self-raising flour
¼ cup (60ml) milk
1 tablespoon icing (confectioners') sugar
brandy yogurt
1½ tablespoons brandy
3 teaspoons light brown sugar
1 cup (280g) greek-style yogurt

1 Preheat oven to 160°C/325°F. Grease 24cm (9½-inch) fluted pie dish.

2 Slice apple thinly; combine in medium bowl with juice. Stir butter, brown sugar and cinnamon in small saucepan over heat until sugar dissolves.

3 Beat extra butter, caster sugar, rind, extract and egg yolks in small bowl with electric mixer until light and fluffy. Stir in sifted flour and milk, in two batches.

4 Beat egg whites in small bowl with electric mixer until soft peaks form; fold into cake mixture, in two batches. Spread mixture into dish.

5 Drain apples; discard juice, return apples to bowl. Stir warm brown sugar mixture into apples. Arrange apple slices over batter in dish; drizzle with brown sugar mixture. Bake about 45 minutes.

6 Meanwhile, make brandy yogurt.

7 Dust milopita with sifted icing sugar; serve warm with brandy yogurt.

brandy yogurt Stir brandy and sugar in small bowl until sugar dissolves; stir in yogurt.

ALLSPICE also called pimento or jamaican pepper; tastes like a combination of nutmeg, cumin, cinnamon and clove. Available whole or ground from most supermarkets and specialty food stores.

ALMONDS

blanched almonds with brown skins removed.

flaked paper-thin slices.

ground also known as almond meal.

slivered small pieces cut lengthways.

ARTICHOKE

hearts tender centre of the globe artichoke; is harvested from the plant after the prickly choke is removed. Cooked hearts can be bought from delis or canned in brine.

BAKING PAPER also called parchment paper or baking parchment; a silicone-coated paper primarily used for lining baking pans and oven trays so cakes and biscuits won't stick.

BAY LEAVES aromatic leaves from the bay tree available fresh or dried; adds a strong, slightly peppery flavour.

BEANS

broad (fava) available dried, fresh, canned and frozen. Peel fresh beans twice – the outer green pod and beige-green inner shell.

BEETROOT (BEETS) firm, round root vegetable.

BICARBONATE OF SODA also called baking soda.

BREADCRUMBS

fresh bread, usually white, processed into crumbs.

stale crumbs made by grating, blending or processing 1- or 2-day-old bread.

BUTTER we use salted butter; 125g is equal to 1 stick (4 ounces).

CAPERS the grey-green buds of a Mediterranean shrub, sold either dried and salted or pickled in a vinegar brine.

CARDAMOM a spice native to India; can be purchased in pod, seed or ground form. Has a distinctive aromatic, sweetly rich flavour.

CAYENNE PEPPER a thin-fleshed, long, extremely hot, dried red chilli, usually purchased ground.

CHEESE

fetta see Greek essentials, page 4.

haloumi see Greek essentials, page 4.

kefalotyri a hard, salty cheese made from sheep and/or goat's milk. Its colour varies from white to yellow depending on the mixture of milk used in the process and its age. Great for grating over pasta or salads. Can be replaced by parmesan.

parmesan also called parmigiano; is a hard, grainy cow's-milk cheese originating in the Parma region of Italy.

CHICKEN

marylands leg and thigh still connected in a single piece; bones and skin intact.

thigh cutlet thigh with skin and centre bone intact; sometimes found skinned with bone intact.

thigh fillet thigh with skin and centre bone removed.

CHICKPEAS (GARBANZO BEANS) also known as hummus or channa; an irregularly round, sandy-coloured legume. It has a firm texture even after cooking, a floury mouth-feel and robust nutty flavour; available canned or dried (reconstitute for several hours in cold water before use).

CHILLI use rubber gloves when seeding and chopping fresh chillies as they can burn your skin. We use unseeded chillies because the seeds contain the heat; use fewer chillies rather than seeding the lot.

CINNAMON available in pieces (sticks or quills) and ground into powder; one of the world's most common spices, used as a sweet, fragrant flavouring for sweet and savoury dishes.

CLOVES dried flower buds of a tropical tree; can be used whole or in ground form. They have a strong scent and taste so should be used sparingly.

COCONUT, DESICCATED concentrated, dried, unsweetened and finely shredded coconut flesh.

CREAM, POURING we use fresh cream, also called pure cream.

CUCUMBER, LEBANESE short, slender and thin-skinned cucumber. Has tender, edible skin, tiny seeds, and sweet, fresh taste.

CUMIN also called zeera or comino; the dried seed of a plant related to the parsley family. It has a spicy, almost curry-like flavour and is available dried as seeds or ground.

CURRANTS, DRIED tiny, almost black raisins so-named after a grape variety that originated in Corinth, Greece. These are not the same as fresh currants, which are the fruit of a plant in the gooseberry family.

DILL used fresh or dried, as seeds or ground, it adds an anise, celery sweetness to foods. Its feathery, frond-like fresh leaves are grassier and more subtle than the dried version or the seeds.

EGGPLANT also called aubergine.

GLOSSARY

EGGS if a recipe calls for raw or barely cooked eggs, exercise caution if there is a salmonella problem in your area, particularly in food eaten by children and pregnant women.

FENNEL also called finocchio or anise; a crunchy green vegetable slightly resembling celery. Is eaten raw, fried or used as an ingredient in soups and sauces. Also the name given to the dried seeds of the plant which have a stronger licorice flavour.

FIGS originally from the countries that border the eastern Mediterranean; are best eaten in peak season, at the height of summer. Vary in skin and flesh colour according to type not ripeness. When ripe, figs should be unblemished and bursting with flesh.

FILLO PASTRY see Greek essentials, page 5.

FLOUR

plain also known as all-purpose.

self-raising plain or wholemeal flour with baking powder and salt added; make at home in the proportion of 1 cup flour to 2 teaspoons baking powder.

HONEY the variety sold in a squeezable container is not suitable for recipes in this book.

KUMARA (ORANGE SWEET POTATO) the Polynesian name of orange-fleshed sweet potato often confused with yam; good baked, boiled, mashed or fried.

LAMB SHANKS forequarter leg; sometimes sold as drumsticks or frenched shanks if gristle and narrow end of the bone are discarded and the remaining meat trimmed.

LENTILS (red, brown, yellow) dried pulses often identified by and named after their colour. Eaten by cultures all over the world, most famously perhaps in the dhals of India, lentils have high food value.

MAPLE-FLAVOURED SYRUP is made from sugar cane and is also known as golden or pancake syrup. It is not a substitute for pure maple syrup.

MAPLE SYRUP, PURE distilled from the sap of sugar maple trees found only in Canada and about ten states in the USA. Maple-flavoured syrup or pancake syrup is not an adequate substitute for the real thing.

NUTMEG a strong and pungent spice. Usually purchased ground, the flavour is more intense freshly grated from the whole nut (available from spice shops).

OIL

cooking-spray we use a cholesterol-free spray made from canola oil.

olive made from ripened olives. Extra virgin and virgin are the first and second press, respectively, of the olives and are therefore considered the best.

vegetable from plant rather than animal fats.

OLIVES, KALAMATA see Greek essentials, page 4.

ONION

green (scallion) also called, incorrectly, shallot; an immature onion picked before the bulb has formed, has a long, bright-green edible stalk.

red also called spanish, red spanish or bermuda onion; a sweet-flavoured, large, purple-red onion.

spring crisp, narrow green-leafed tops and a round sweet white bulb larger than green onions.

OREGANO a herb, also called wild marjoram; has a woody stalk and clumps of tiny, dark-green leaves. Has a pungent, peppery flavour.

ORZO a small rice-sized pasta. It can be replaced with risoni which is slightly smaller.

OUZO an aniseed-flavoured Greek spirit.

PANCETTA an Italian unsmoked bacon. Used, sliced or chopped as an ingredient rather than eaten on its own.

PAPRIKA ground dried sweet red capsicum (bell pepper); also available sweet, hot, mild and smoked.

PINE NUTS also known as pignoli; not a nut but a small, cream-coloured kernel from pine cones. They are best roasted before use to bring out the flavour.

PITTA BREAD also called lebanese bread. A wheat-flour pocket bread sold in large, flat pieces that separate into rounds. Also available in small pieces called pocket pitta.

POLENTA also called cornmeal; a flour-like cereal made of dried corn (maize). Also the dish made from it.

POTATOES

desiree oval, smooth and pink-skinned, waxy yellow flesh; good boiled, roasted and in salads.

kipfler (fingerling) finger-shaped, nutty flavour; good in salads.

sebago white skin, oval; good fried, mashed and baked.

RICE

arborio small, round-grain rice well-suited to absorb a large amount of liquid; the high level of starch makes it suitable for risottos.

basmati a white, fragrant long-grained rice; the grains fluff up when cooked. It should be washed several times before cooking.

RIGANI see Greek essentials, page 4.

RISONI small rice-shaped pasta; similar to another small pasta, orzo.

ROASTING/TOASTING spread nuts and dried coconut evenly on oven tray; roast in moderate oven about 5 minutes. Stir desiccated coconut, pine nuts and sesame seeds over low heat in heavy-based frying pan to toast more evenly.

ROCKET (ARUGULA) also called rugula and rucola; peppery green leaf eaten raw in salads or used in cooking. Baby rocket leaves are smaller and less peppery.

SAFFRON the stigma of a member of the crocus family, available ground or in strands; imparts a yellow-orange colour to food once infused. The quality can vary greatly; the best is the world's most expensive spice.

SEAFOOD

mussels should only be bought from a reliable fish market: they must be tightly closed when bought, indicating they are alive. Before cooking, scrub shells with a strong brush and remove the beards; do not eat any that do not open after cooking. Varieties include black and green-lip.

octopus are usually tenderised before you buy them; both octopus and squid require either long slow cooking (usually for large molluscs) or quick cooking over high heat (usually for small molluscs) – anything in between will make the octopus tough and rubbery.

prawns (shrimp) can be purchased cooked or uncooked (green), with or without shells.

squid also called calamari; a type of mollusc. Buy squid hoods to make preparation and cooking faster.

white fish fillets means fillets from non-oily fish; includes bream, whiting, ling, flathead, snapper, dhufish and redfish.

SEMOLINA coarsely ground flour milled from durum wheat; the flour used in making gnocchi, pasta and couscous.

SESAME SEEDS black and white are the most common of this small oval seed. The seeds are used as an ingredient and as a condiment. Roast in a heavy-based frying pan over low heat.

SHALLOTS also called french shallots, golden shallots or eschalots. Small and elongated, with a brown-skin, they grow in tight clusters similar to garlic.

SILVER BEET (SWISS CHARD) also called, incorrectly, spinach; has fleshy stalks and large leaves, both of which can be prepared as for spinach.

SOUR CREAM a thick, commercially-cultured sour cream with a minimum fat content of 35 per cent.

SPINACH also called english spinach and, incorrectly, silver beet.

SPLIT PEAS yellow or green varieties, both with a sweet, strong pea flavour. They are usually pre-soaked but may be cooked without soaking.

SUGAR

brown, light a soft, finely granulated sugar retaining molasses for its colour and flavour.

caster (superfine) finely granulated table sugar.

TAHINI see Greek essentials, page 5.

TOMATO

bottled pasta sauce a prepared sauce; a blend of tomatoes, herbs and spices.

paste triple-concentrated tomato puree used to flavour soups, stews and sauces.

puree canned pureed tomatoes (not tomato paste).

VANILLA

bean dried, long, thin pod; the minuscule black seeds inside are used to impart a vanilla flavour in baking and desserts.

extract obtained from vanilla beans infused in water; a non-alcoholic version of essence.

VINE LEAVES see Greek essentials, page 5.

VINEGAR

balsamic originally from Modena, Italy, there are now many balsamic vinegars on the market ranging in pungency and quality. Quality can be determined up to a point by price; use the most expensive sparingly.

cider made from fermented apples.

WATERCRESS one of the cress family, a large group of peppery greens used raw in salads, dips and sandwiches, or cooked in soups. Highly perishable, so it must be used shortly after purchase.

YEAST (dried and fresh), a raising agent. Granular (7g sachets) and fresh compressed (20g blocks) yeast can usually be substituted for each other.

YOGURT, GREEK see Greek essentials, page 5.

ZUCCHINI also called courgette.

CONVERSION CHART

MEASURES

One Australian metric measuring cup holds approximately 250ml, one Australian metric tablespoon holds 20ml, one Australian metric teaspoon holds 5ml.

The difference between one country's measuring cups and another's is within a 2- or 3-teaspoon variance, and will not affect your cooking results. North America, New Zealand and the United Kingdom use a 15ml tablespoon. All cup and spoon measurements are level. The most accurate way of measuring dry ingredients is to weigh them. When measuring liquids, use a clear glass or plastic jug with metric markings.

We use large eggs with an average weight of 60g.

DRY MEASURES

METRIC	IMPERIAL
15g	½oz
30g	1oz
60g	2oz
90g	3oz
125g	4oz (¼lb)
155g	5oz
185g	6oz
220g	7oz
250g	8oz (½lb)
280g	9oz
315g	10oz
345g	11oz
375g	12oz (¾lb)
410g	13oz
440g	14oz
470g	15oz
500g	16oz (1lb)
750g	24oz (1½lb)
1kg	32oz (2lb)

LIQUID MEASURES

METRIC	IMPERIAL
30ml	1 fluid oz
60ml	2 fluid oz
100ml	3 fluid oz
125ml	4 fluid oz
150ml	5 fluid oz
190ml	6 fluid oz
250ml	8 fluid oz
300ml	10 fluid oz
500ml	16 fluid oz
600ml	20 fluid oz
1000ml (1 litre)	1¾ pints

LENGTH MEASURES

METRIC	IMPERIAL
3mm	⅛in
6mm	¼in
1cm	½in
2cm	¾in
2.5cm	1in
5cm	2in
6cm	2½in
8cm	3in
10cm	4in
13cm	5in
15cm	6in
18cm	7in
20cm	8in
23cm	9in
25cm	10in
28cm	11in
30cm	12in (1ft)

OVEN TEMPERATURES

These oven temperatures are only a guide for conventional ovens.
For fan-forced ovens, check the manufacturer's manual.

	°C (CELSIUS)	°F (FAHRENHEIT)
Very slow	120	250
Slow	150	275-300
Moderately slow	160	325
Moderate	180	350-375
Moderately hot	200	400
Hot	220	425-450
Very hot	240	475

The imperial measurements used in these recipes are approximate only. Measurements for cake pans are approximate only.

A

almond and walnut pastries
(kataifi) 65
almond biscuits 67

B

baby octopus, barbecued 10
baby calamari, deep-fried 11
baklava 62
biscuits, almond 67
brandy yogurt 73
broad beans and artichokes 58

C

cabbage salad 24
cake, yogurt 71
capsicum
char-grilled capsicum
salad 32
goat and capsicum stew 51
char-grilled capsicum salad 32
cheese
fetta 4
haloumi 4
herbed fetta cheese 15
pan-fried haloumi 14
sauce 43
spinach and fetta salad 24
watermelon and haloumi
salad 22
cherry spoon sweet 70
chicken
chicken, lemon and
rice soup 18
grilled lemon 38
roasted garlic, lemon and
oregano 37

D

dip, eggplant 16
dolmades 6
dressing
pickled red onion 22
tomato 58

E

eggplant
deep-fried with herb
sauce 11
dip 16
moussaka 40

F

fetta cheese 4
herbed 15
spinach and fetta salad 24
fig galettes 66
fillo pastry 5
baklava 62
spanakopita 13

G

galaktoboureko 68
garlic and lemon potatoes 26
garlic and lemon yogurt 8
goat and capsicum stew 51
greek coffee 66
greek essentials 4–5
greek salad 25
greek-style yogurt 5
brandy yogurt 73
garlic and lemon yogurt 8
green beans, braised 54

H

haloumi cheese 4
pan-fried 14
watermelon and haloumi
salad 22
halva 60

K

kalamata olives 4
thyme and garlic 14
kataifi (almond and walnut
pastries) 65
kebabs, lemon and garlic
lamb 47

L

lamb
baked lamb shanks
with orzo 48
barbecued lamb
sandwiches 52
fried lamb meatballs 10
lemon and garlic lamb
kebabs 47
moussaka 40
pastitsio 43
slow-roasted with skordalia
and potatoes 44
lemon and garlic lamb
kebabs 47
lemon syrup 65, 68

M

mezze
barbecued baby octopus 10
deep-fried baby calamari 11
deep-fried eggplant with herb
sauce 11
deep-fried zucchini balls 15
dolmades 6
fried chilli prawns with garlic
and lemon yogurt 8
fried lamb meatballs 10
herbed fetta cheese 15
pan-fried haloumi 14
skordalia 16
spanakopita 13
taramasalata 17
thyme and garlic olives 14
tzatziki 17
milopita 73
moussaka 40
mussel and orzo broth 21

O

olives
kalamata 4
thyme and garlic 14
orange spoon sweet 70

INDEX

P

pastitsio 43
pastry
  fillo 5
  spanakopita 13
pickled red onion dressing 22
pickled zucchini salad 25
potatoes
  garlic and lemon 26
  slow-cooked potatoes with wine
    and herbs 56
  slow-roasted lamb with skordalia
    and potatoes 44
prawn souvlakia with tomato and
  fennel sauce 31

R

rabbit stifado 34
rigani 4
  roasted garlic, lemon and
    oregano chicken 37

S

salad
  cabbage 24
  char-grilled capsicum 32
  greek 25
  pickled zucchini 25
  spinach and fetta 24
  watermelon and haloumi salad 22
sauce
  cheese 43
  deep-fried eggplant with herb
    sauce 11
  meat 43
  tomato and fennel 31
  white 40
seafood
  barbecued baby octopus 10
  barbecued vine-leaf-wrapped
    sardines 26
  deep-fried baby calamari 11
  fried chilli prawns with garlic and
    lemon yogurt 8

mussel and orzo broth 21
oven-baked fish with tomato
  and olives 28
prawn souvlakia with tomato
  and fennel sauce 31
tuna souvlakia with char-grilled
  capsicum salad 32
skordalia 16, 44
  slow-roasted lamb with skordalia
    and potatoes 44
soup
  chicken, lemon and rice 18
  mussel and orzo broth 21
spanakopita 13
spinach and fetta salad 24
stew, goat and capsicum 51
sweets
  almond and walnut pastries
    (kataifi) 65
  almond biscuits 67
  baklava 62
  caramelised figs & yogurt 71
  cherry spoon sweet 70
  fig galettes 66
  galaktoboureko 68
  greek coffee 66
  halva 60
  milopita 73
  orange spoon sweet 70
  spiced plums with yogurt 67
  yogurt cake 71
syrup 65
  lemon 65, 68

T

tahini 5
taramasalata 17
thyme and garlic olives 14
tomato and fennel
  sauce 31
tomato dressing 58
tuna souvlakia with char-grilled
  capsicum salad 32
tzatziki 17

V

vegetable dishes
  braised green beans 54
  broad beans and artichokes 58
  slow-cooked potatoes with wine
    and herbs 56
vine leaves 5
  barbecued vine-leaf-wrapped
    sardines 26
  dolmades 6

W

watermelon and haloumi salad 22
white sauce 40

Y

yogurt
  brandy 73
  cake 71
  garlic and lemon 8
  greek-style 5

Z

zucchini
  pickled zucchini salad 25
  zucchini balls, deep-fried 15

First published in 2012 by ACP Books, Sydney

ACP Books are published by ACP Magazines Limited

a division of Nine Entertainment Co.

54 Park St, Sydney

GPO Box 4088, Sydney, NSW 2001.

phone (+61)2 9282 8618; fax (+61)2 9126 3702

acpbooks@acpmagazines.com.au; www.acpbooks.com.au

ACP BOOKS

General Manager - Christine Whiston

Editor-in-Chief - Susan Tomnay

Creative Director - Hieu Chi Nguyen

Food Director - Pamela Clark

Published and distributed in the United Kingdom by Octopus Publishing Group

Endeavour House

189 Shaftesbury Avenue

London WC2H 8JY

United Kingdom

phone (+44)(0)207 632 5400; fax (+44)(0)207 632 5405

info@octopus-publishing.co.uk;

www.octopusbooks.co.uk

Printed by Toppan Printing Co., China

International foreign language rights, Brian Cearnes, ACP Books bcearnes@acpmagazines.com.au

A catalogue record for this book is available from the British Library.

ISBN 978-1-907428-39-5